Moments

With

Melissa Sherry Smith's

5th grade Class

By

Joanne Sherry Mitchell

BOOKS BY JOANNE SHERRY MITCHELL

Moments
Moments And Then Some
Moments When Night Becomes Day
Moments Gentle Hints to Life
Moments Not Things
Moments No Replacement Found
Moments With Melissa Sherry Smith's 5th Grade Class

Visit Joanne Mitchell's website

www.momentsbyjoanne.com

You may email her

at

moments@momentsbyjoanne.com

Printed in the United States of America.

ACKNOWLEDGEMENTS

Cover Art self-description by the fifth-grade students of Melissa Sherry Smith's class.

Design edits for cover by Victor Morales, Art Director Professional Management, Inc.

With special thanks for their continual assistance in completing this book to:

Betty Smith

Marie Bartlett

ACKNOWLEDGEMENTS

A special thank you to:

Melissa Sherry Smith, 5th Grade Teacher at
Vista Lake Elementary School, with her family.

The talented 5th Graders of
Of Vista Lake Elementary School
True Artists in the making who made my
Poems magically come to life.

ILLUSTRATIONS

This book is dedicated

to

Elinor Cleare

My Sister

Who always welcomed me

In her home and

Took the role of

Mother #2

P.S. Thanks for worrying so much

so I don't have to worry

Contents

GHOSTS

Not sure they are real

For I have not seen one

Yet I know they are around

Especially late at night,

When all are asleep

They wake me up

Want to play

Or scare me;

Mostly scare me.

I have not learned

How to play with

Ghosts that visit me

In the middle

Of the night

When the wind

Is speaking

As loud as my heart is

Beating.

JOBS

What do I want to be

When I grow up

I have been asked that question so many times.

I really do not know

I can say fireman, policeman, teacher, doctor, dentist;

I do not like any of those

I would rather say to all the adults that ask me

I have not made up my mind yet.

I wish I knew what I want to be when I grow up

Some of my friends already know what they want to be

One of my friends has the crazy idea of

Being a hotel critic

He says he wants to travel, but does not have the money

By going to hotels and acting as a critic, he can see what's going on

Find what's dirty, find what's not working.

He stays at the hotel he is reviewing for free

Seems like a good way to travel.

Not for me, I like a home and my bedroom

If I had that job, I would be away all the time.

My dad is an apartment manager

I do not want to follow in his footsteps

There always seems to be an emergency

Roof is leaking

Someone fell down the elevator shaft.

The emergency seems to come

In the middle of the night

Or when we sit down for dinner.

At twelve, I think I am old enough

To tell anyone that asks what I want to be

My answer is, I have not decided yet.

If they want to listen to me

I can tell them what I do not want

It's going to be a process of elimination

Until I know.

WHEN I WAS YOUNGER

There are happenings

That stay with me

Which I will not forget

I am sitting in my highchair

Mom gave me a bowl of peaches

They tasted so good

I started licking the bowl

At the moment I was licking

Syrup of the peaches

With such enjoyment

A repair man came into the kitchen;

Started laughing at me

Embarrassed for the first time.

Gabby

GONE

We were swimming in the ocean

I was about ten

The waves were high

Brothers and I

Riding the waves in

For a while

Laughing, choking on the water

Looking for the biggest wave;

The best ride.

Well, my bathing suit came off

I went underwater

To find my new red bathing suit

It's hard to open your eyes

Under the surf in salt water

I did it because I had to

Nowhere in sight my pretty red bathing suit

Wave covering me, no longer able to ride

The big waves

Now I had to figure out how to get to my

Towel or shirt, something

No luck

I had to walk, no, I ran

To our blanket

Naked;

Embarrassed;

Wet and cold.

THE MOON

To be watched

It moves

It grows, it shrinks

It grows again.

In the middle of the night

The golden glow is bright as sunrise

Coming through my bedroom window

I'm

Always watching the moon

When it rises it looks like

A monster coming out of the sea

No monster at all;

It's the bright golden glow of our full moon.

No sun, wind, or rain can take the moon away

It comes back ever so slowly each month

I can see this big moon anywhere I go

At home

In the park

Oh yes, the moon joined us in

New York City

Our moon dances all month long;

Tells my brain good things last.

SCIENCE FAIR

Which I dislike

I got to come up with something

To test

To invent

To make.

Last year at the Science Fair

Kids made things

Like how the toilet works, which was

Pretty interesting

Understanding how a toilet works through pictures

Because of gravity.

Even though we all know the toilet

The kids and I laughed about how simple

The toilet is, yet we use it every day.

Two things I find I like

Flying in space in a rocket

Everyday people can now go into space

And the other is, noise

My dad will not let me have music on

When doing my homework

Not prepare for the next blastoff
I would love to prove to my dad
I can do homework with music
My music of course
As if it were quiet.
I asked a few of my friends
To do the same math problems
In the quiet and with music
They did the same math problems
Both times, I just mixed up the order
Interesting, the results which I did seven times
Without music, more problems were right
With music they worked faster, less
Problems right.
Conclusion was, music helps me get going
Quiet help me have perfect answers
This Science Fair was fun for a change
I won my blue ribbon
I still like music with homework
Little embarrassing;
Dad was right.

MONEY

I like having money

So does my mom and dad

They always say

Watch what you spend

Money does not grow on trees.

They are right, I never

Saw money hanging on

The oak trees in our back yard

I think it grows in banks or in the

Cards, credit cards Mom and Dad carry

With them all the time.

Somehow, they pay for everything

With those skinny cards in their wallets.

Saturday Dad and I went to buy

My soccer uniform

When we found what I needed

We waited in line to pay for my soccer uniforms.

Dad took out this little card

No money, just the card

I did not see any money

You know the green dollars

We get as presents?

Dad explained he gets money from working

The money goes into the bank

I pay all my bills from the money I put in the bank, he said

Each month the credit card company sends me a bill

I pay the bill with the money the bank is holding.

Like when we play monopoly

The bank holds the money

The work is going around the game board

I buy property, collect rent, hopefully to win.

Money has importance to buy things

I like the idea of making money from rents

Like in the game Monopoly.

Somehow, I have to figure out how to make money

By investing, working, and saving

I am going to start like my dad, when I get money

I want a bank account to save my money for

What I want, what I need and give a little to Mom.

I HAVE LEARNED

How to deal with kids in my class

I am steadfast with doing right.

When there is a choice to be made

I choose as if my dad

Is sitting on my shoulder

I try to do as he would want me to do.

The thing I have trouble with

Is my brain

Sometimes my brain acts

Like it dislikes me

As an enemy does

I have a war going on in my head

Studying for a test

I know I should;

Riding my bike is so much fun.

Last night instead of studying for the

Spelling test

I rode my bike

Around the neighborhood

I got a bad grade.

I tell myself, listen

How stupid

You have all the answers to the spelling test

That is the "one" test you should always study for

You have all the answers to make a hundred;

That is the war I have going on in my brain

The part of me that cannot be my enemy

I have to work with my brain and do

What is right for the man on my shoulder

My dad.

MONDAY

The start of the week

I need help to get going

Cookies

That's what will help me

Not just one

I have to have at least five.

Monday is the hardest day

To get up

Knowing I have five days

Of

Homework

Tests

Reading

Math

Learning

Five big warm

Chocolate chip cookies

Gets me going.

october
school
cook

I HAVE DECIDED

To take better care of my puppy

Mom and Dad tell me

I am immature

Too immature to have pets.

I like pets

They keep me warm on cold nights

I can take puppy dog for walks

Meet all

Types of people and kids in my neighborhood

I see some strange things in nature

Spiders, bees and today I saw a hawk.

I dislike picking up his poop

Yet I do the clean up

I like his name-

Puppy Dog.

Everyone I talk to

Smiles when they hear his name

Puppy Dog.

ONLY TWO TYPES

Of people

Good ones and bad ones

I decided to hang out

With the good ones

That's the right answer

I really know this

Yet

Sometimes I find myself

Hanging out with the bad ones

Not so good.

EXPLORING

On our raft

We lived on the Seaboard Canal

Which flowed into the Miami River.

We were given a raft

By the workman

On Captain Hans's boat

They were done and

Had no need of their raft.

Four large empty oil barrels

Kept our raft afloat

With plywood for our deck

For oars we used

Swimming flippers

Cut palm tree branches.

Now the lucky part in my life

I had brothers, sisters

All willing to go exploring

With me, on the Seaboard Canal

We got on our raft

With jars of water

A few snacks

Full of joy

For

The adventure that awaited us.

The current took us all the way

To the Miami River

That's when the trouble started

With all our power

Of hard continuous rowing

We could not get back home;

The current was too strong.

We got so tired of paddling

We had to stop

Let the current take us farther away

From home.

We drank all our water

Ate all our snacks

Exploring turned out to frighten us

Lucky for us

A boat came along

We cried for help

They tied us to their boat

Brought us back home.

We loved our adventure

Yet glad to be back home

On the journey

We saw woods uninhabited

On the Miami River.

Our next adventure

Travel the river

Dock our boat, so we can

Explore the uninhabited woods

Hopefully, the current will work with us.

ROACHES

The roaches of the night

Silently roam

Fast crawlers

They can hide in the

Tiniest of cracks

In brown paper bags

Cardboard boxes

Surprise you when

You open your dresser drawer

Expecting to pull out your t-shirt

Out comes that big ugly

Roach

Scares the heck out of me.

Those big ugly roaches

Eat every little crumb left on the table

Yet

They're no bigger than an inch

Yes

As scary as a ghost.

CROSS OVERS

What do you have when

You cross an iguana

With a bird?

A small flying dragon

Frightfully ugly.

Cross a poodle with a hen?

A curly-haired loud noise maker.

What do you have when you cross

A tall handsome man

With a cute blonde-haired woman?

Me.

Thanks, Mom and Dad.

INVENTIONS

I hate to read

Yet I love the stories in books.

That should be the next

Invention;

Reading by osmosis.

Every word

All your homework

The entire book

Put into your brain

Knowledge and ideas

Just for the asking;

No need to read.

You just ask this

New invention

To put into your head all the information

Of what you have to read.

Hopefully Mom

Or Dad

Will buy me the

Invention when invented.

JOURNALS

My teacher suggested

We write journals

Everyday.

No one will read it

According to my teacher.

The journal is to

Think about who you are

Who you want to be

How life treats you.

Like yesterday

Friends hurt me

In the lunch room

No room left at our usual table

No one would move over

To

Make room

For me.

I decided I am leaving my journal

In the open

I want everyone to know how I feel

What I want

How I get hurt

Maybe just maybe

I will be understood better

By everyone getting to know me

Through my journal.

I GOT AN "A"

On my last test

I think to myself

I did good

Mom and Dad

Loved the A paper.

First thing I think

With an A, I can take it easy

Wasn't easy to read a book and

Write about it.

Figure out while

I am writing

What made it a good book

Study for the test on the book

With the A, I can rest

Not study as hard

Maybe not do all my homework.

No

That does not work

Everyone will be after me.

It's not about what I have done

It's that I have a long way to go

Getting to where I want to go

My responsibility;

One test at a time.

MARS

I want to visit Mars

After the moon visit

We are going to be able to travel

Throughout space

Without all the training

Astronauts do.

Space X did it last year

Today I know Mars has two moons

There are so many stories about Mars

When I go

I will find out

What stories are real or made up.

Yes, one day I will be on Mars

As easy as it is to visit my uncle

In New York City.

mars

MY GODFATHER

Is a chief at The Plaza

It's a grand old hotel

In New York City.

Last week, he came to our home for a visit

We are going to make apple pie

I will teach you how simple

Baking a pie is, he said.

Then he asks me

Would you like that?

For sure, learning to cook

So far, I know how to make eggs

French toast, and hot dogs.

I love our kitchen

So much happens in the kitchen

It's where we have the best of times

Over the dinner table.

My godfather says,

First, we have to see if we have the right tools

To bake apple pie

Make a list of ingredients to buy.

Never thought about it, we need tools to bake
Different, I am guessing, from scrambling eggs.
We make the list together
He tells me to write down what we do not have
He has nothing written, he is sitting in the chair.
I have the pencil and paper
He starts to list ingredients we need
Look and see if you have four sticks of butter
We have that, okay
Cinnamon, at least four large spoons full
We have that. no need to write it out.
He tells me what we need
I find it in the kitchen
The only item we do not have
Is a rolling pin and a baking dish in the shape of a pie
Which we go buy.
Now Theo, what I call my godfather,
Chases everyone out of the kitchen
We have to have silence while we create.
I'm excited
I know the best thing about apple pie is the eating

We start with the crust

Flour all over the place

Mom is going to have a fit when she sees the mess

We are making;

Flour goes everywhere with little help.

We make four balls of dough for the crust

He gets white cotton material

Spreads it out, we get the rolling pin and

This little ball becomes flat and round for the crust of the pie.

Rolling pin is like a toy

We put a damp cloth on the crust while we peel the apples;

Big red apples.

That is the hardest part, peeling about

Thirty-five apples

We cut them in slices and throw all the pits away

We keep the skin for apple juice he says we will make

While the pies are cooking.

I just love how he measures everything with his hands

No measuring cups or spoons, everything is done

With hands and feel.

I love making the crust in thin stripes for the pie's top

So easy, the slices of peeled apples go into the baking dish

We add a whole stick of butter, with sugar and cinnamon

Again, no measuring.

He asks me to smell the cinnamon and butter;

Smells great.

Then, I put the strips of crust on the top

Goes in the oven.

You guessed it, the best

Apple pie I ever had!

I can still make it the same way

No measuring cups

Although now I have to clean my mess.

MY FIFTH-GRADE TEACHER

I like her

Tall and soft spoken

She has been in this classroom

For five years.

Kids, my age

Have sat at this desk before

I know kids will sit at my desk

After I am gone

My fifth-grade teacher

Will be here.

A brave teacher

She stands in front of us

Every day of school

Never knowing what will happen

In our classroom.

One day two birds flew in the classroom

She had to figure out how to get them out

Before they go to the bathroom

On all or just one of us.

Within seconds, they went to the bathroom

On Mikey's desk.

Miss Sherry, my fifth-grade teacher

Asked us all to stand in one

Corner of the classroom

Holding up our hands

She told us to sing.

"Ring Around the Roses"

With our hands in the air

We formed a straight line

And moved slowly toward the birds

They move away from us

Closer to the window

We kept singing, waving our hands, high in the air

Finally, the birds flew out the window.

Another day we hear

Over the loud speaker in our room

They rang bells and told us to

Walk as quickly as we can

Down the nearest steps

Continue until we are outside

I was a bit frightened, what was happening?

Miss Sherry helped us line up

Telling us not to worry, just follow directions

When we are outside, I will make sure

We all know what is happening, she said.

We could not go back into the school

For three days, there was a gas leak

Dangerous for all of us.

Miss Sherry was ready to teach

The day we got back to the classroom.

BACKYARD SQUIRRELS

Which I have a few of.

When in bed early morning

I watch the squirrels

Jump from tree to tree

Eating the bird seeds I put out.

I know the food is for the birds

It's ok with me

I like the squirrels

Jumping from tree to tree

Up, down each branch of the tree.

My science teacher told me they love oak trees;

I have one right outside my bedroom window.

One warm morning, this brown squirrel

Carried a branch

Twice his size

To a location high in the tree.

An amazing path to

Carry one branch to its destination

Then back down,

He was biting off

Another branch

Back up the tree, to the place he had decided to build

The family nest.

After four or five branches

The nest is built and

My squirrel is out of sight

I want to help be part of the growing family.

I think and decide

The growing family will need food

So, I put a second bird feeder in the tree

My plan is to keep watching

While making sure the bird feeder is always filled.

WORRYING CAT

I got up earlier than needed

I was worried

That I forgot to do all my homework

I double-checked

Figured out, I did it all

Yeah.

Worrying over homework

Is ridiculous, to have

A nightmare about homework

Especially when I finished

All my homework.

I wonder if my cat worries?

He acts just like a human

Lots of times

I think it's cute.

He acts like a human

When

He rubs up against my leg

I know he wants something.

Similar, to the way I help my mom

A little more than I have to

If I want a special gift

For my birthday.

Now do I have a

Worrying cat?

For I am

A worrying cat.

RAINBOW

Today reaches across the sky

To places I have not gone.

Colors so bright and inviting

To a journey I will make

To places yet unseen by me.

The rainbow with its bands of colors

Wrapping the present of my tomorrows

For me to open.

The rainbow never hiding

Always inviting

Makes today a good day

Thinking, dreaming of all the places

I will be.

Aliyah

FAMILY TIME

This weekend I went

With the whole family to

A wedding

All eight of us in one car

It's a bit crowded.

In the car

Mom would only let us have one bag

To take with us

We had to pack it ourselves

And carry it ourselves.

How do I know what to pack?

I ask Dad what he is taking

Since we are both men.

He would know, he goes out of town

For work several times a year.

He tells me

We are going for three days

You will need enough to wear for three days

One outfit per day

Sounds reasonable.

The most important item I take

Is shoes

I cannot do anything with shoes that hurt,

When you travel you walk a lot.

I look in my drawers

Too many things to bring

Undershirts, underpants, sweater, shorts

Socks, pants, the fancy outfit for the wedding.

How do I get all that in one suitcase?

Then I want to take my iPad with me

I go to Mom, maybe she has some other ideas

She says put everything you want to take on your bed

And see if it fits in the suitcase

If it does not fit

You have to start taking things out

Okay, I will try that.

Three days, three outfits

I start making piles on the bed

Of clothes, my stuff animals, and my favorite blanket

Not everything fits

I have to repack.

I start with the most important item to me

My favorite blanket and stuff monkey

Never go to sleep

Without them,

Then I take Dad's advice, I put in my most comfortable shoes

That was easy, I only have one pair

Mom yells, make sure you put in the outfit you're wearing to the

Wedding first.

Okay, I do that I have a little room left

I put pajamas back, I will wear to bed what I wear during the day

Underwear and t-shirts I pack three of each

Then, I only have room for one pair of shorts, two shirts.

My sister yells, do not forget your comb, toothpaste and brush

Okay, there is room for the little things

I'm packed, ready to go.

The car ride is hard, seven hours, all in one little box it seems

Dad and Mom are comfortable, they are in the front

With windows, better air conditioning, we are in the back

Drawing imaginary lines to separate us, from one another

We make it to my aunts and uncle's home

They are ready for us

We get to dive in their pool, have watermelon and small sandwiches.

We play with all the other cousins

There are nineteen of us in all.

The wedding was long, boring;

The food and games were fun.

Best of all, I cannot wait to be with my whole family again

My uncle is going to set up a Zoom cousin fest, on

The sixteenth day

Of every month, to say hi to each other.

Family time on Zoom

Better than school on Zoom.

THE CHRISTMAS I CRIED

I am thirteen years old

I love getting presents

So much fun, not knowing

What you will get as a gift.

I love the pretty wrappings

The little gift cards.

It's Christmas morning

I sit around the tree

With my whole family

A perfect moment to be

A kid

Although I am not going to be a kid

Too much longer

Thirteen is the start of being a teenager.

Everyone is getting gifts

Grandma saves everything

She is opening her present

Saving the ribbon, the bow, the pretty
Red foil paper
Then, I get a plain white envelope
No card, no box, no ribbon
A card, that holds money
Two twenty-dollar bills
With the words
Merry Christmas Robert
Love Aunt Helen and Uncle Jim
Well, that is all I got
Five, yes five
Cards with money this Christmas
I was looking forward to games
A book, something other than money.
I start to cry
Me, a thirteen-year-old
Disappointed at Christmas.

HIDE

I found my spot to hide

It's in my closet.

Lucky for me

I have three things

A closet

A door to the closet

A rechargeable flashlight.

Matter of fact, the flashlight

Has a crank when the light goes out

I crank the handle, for a little time

The light comes back on.

I hide mostly to read

The perfect spot

It's quiet

My little brother cannot open the door

I read, until I get tired or

I have to go to the bathroom

Which I hate to do, sometimes

I am at a great part of the book

I have to stop something I like doing

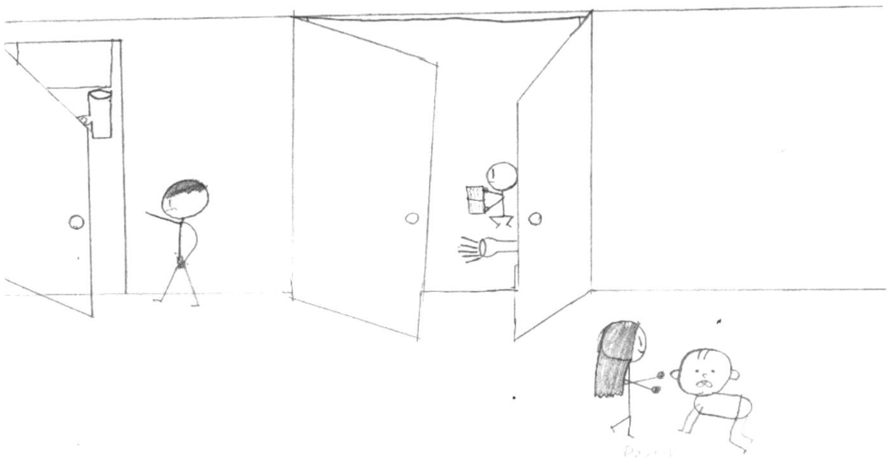

To do something, I got to do.

Sometimes Mom calls me

To set the table for dinner

Go play outside with friends

A busy life I have.

Opening a new book for the first time

Brings me joy, for I do not know

Where my new book will take me;

What I will learn.

The place I hide lets me concentrate

No one, no sound

Just me, my book

And the

Flashlight.

DRONES

Drones

Turn off any technology

That is making a sound

Close your eyes

Take a deep breath

Inhale to the count of eight.

Hold your breath to the count of five

Exhale to the count of eight

Now, you are ready to imagine

Believe in your dreams

Soar like the drones

With you in control of

Your new adventures

With all the possibilities.

WHITE SHIRT

I wear

Eating out.

First thing

I drop a drop

Of food on the white shirt

Large enough

For all to see.

My shirt is no longer white

Maybe, if I keep eating

Keep dropping food

It will be white with red polka dots

With tasty red spaghetti sauce.

TODAY

We are iguanas

Looking

For a place to hide,

A place to call home.

Someone filled-in my home with rocks.

I know it was only a hole in the ground

Yet

It was cozy and warmed

By the morning sun.

Today

I climb the big old oak tree,

It's fun to go to the top

And look around.

I see the perfect place

To dig my new home.

Nick

IDLE

My Dad loved to see me doing something

He encouraged us to be busy

With helping around the house

Helping people who couldn't do for themselves

Like Mrs. Henry.

I had to help her with her groceries every Saturday

Matter of fact, Dad hated

Idle hands.

Today Dad sees a lot of

Idle hands

Playing games, talking on the phone

Texting, viewing Tik Tok.

Technology, never Dad's idea of

Solving the dilemma of idleness.

Yesterday, Dad and I

Worked in the yard

Cutting down a tree that died

I had to learn how to use an ax.

First of all, let me tell you

An ax is heavy
My arms had to swing from over my shoulder
To the opposite side of my body
The tree started to lean after twenty swings
Already I am a bit tired.
Dad and I had to figure out
Where the tree was to fall
Wanted to make sure, it wasn't going to hit
Us or our home
We tied a rope on the tree, dad pulling it to
The safe side of the yard
I kept swinging
I stopped counting the swings
Getting tired now.
The tree finally fell
Hit no one
Missed our home.
I felt like I won a prize
When the job was done.

THE DARK SIDE

The moon has a dark side

Never knew what was going on

At the dark side of the moon.

Only

When in space

We can see

The dark side

The secrets of space unlocking

Before us.

Yesterday, we landed on the moon

Tomorrow, it's Mars, the stars

Meeting new creatures

Unknowing what is in store.

Outer space, so vast

Hard to believe there are

No other life forms.

Our tiny sparks of

Imagination

Grow, with each new

Discovery.

The brave, the curious

Will venture out.

BETTY CAN WHISTLE

Linda can sing like a lark

Elinor can make the best meatballs

Jeannie can hide so no one can find her

Chris can paint anything so it looks real

Alex can make the computer do all sorts of tricks

John can act like a ghost and scare anybody or anyone

Melissa can teach a dog tricks with a whisper.

My brothers and sisters

We practice what we are best at each day

Betty is sitting on the front porch

A shadow appears

Jennie shows us the best place to hide

Elinor has baked the best meatballs

The shadow stops, to have a taste

While he is listening to the song and eating

The world's best meatballs.

Linda sings her best

The shadow stops, right in his tracks to listen.

Betty starts to whistle

Warns us danger is approaching

As the shadow grows near.

Alex sends an email for help.

Melissa teaches our puppy dog to bark

So loud, the shadow

Walks backwards into

The door

Chris has painted.

The door looks open, there is no door so

The shadow bangs right into the wall.

John, our family ghost, blows up as big as an elephant and

Blows the shadow out of the house.

We laugh

We are safe

Laughing hard enough

To scare our fears away.

WORD

The word that gives magic

To our story

Hehehehohohololololomomomonaaweaweaweee

The word that opens doors

Serves ice cream

Repeat after me

Hehehehahahalolololomomomonaaweaweaweee

No need for a wand

No need for a rabbit's foot

No need for a fairy godmother;

Nice to have one.

With this magic word

You only need to say

Hehehehahahalolololomomomonaaweaweaweee

Memorize the word

For you never know

When a little magic is needed.

In the middle of the night

My magic word can

Stop thunder and lightning

Can rid my room of ghosts

Place a blanket on me when it’s cold.

Remember the word

Hehehehahahalolololomomomonaaweaweaweee.

THE JOB

Being something

Being someone

What to choose.

Plenty to choose from

Some days I want to be someone

Silly and simple

Like the balloon man.

Not even sure there is something like a balloon man

I know we can buy balloons all blown up

At every food store in town.

What if, I was a balloon man

I would go to parks

Sell fifty balloons in a day

Of all colors

Bright and full of air, that

Floats the balloons

Like magic to little kids.

I know, it's a special gas

But little kids do not understand.

I will give them wonder

Of the floating balloons

In all sizes, shapes and colors

The joy I will bring to kids.

I will figure out

How to return a balloon that floated

High into the sky.

The job Drew by Khloe-

I LIKE BALLOONS

No, I love balloons

They are fun to fill with water

The fights Mom, Dad, my brothers and sisters

Have

Filling up the balloon with water

Throwing the filled balloon in the air

Hoping it lands in the right place

Not to hurt, just to wet.

We run and duck

Laughing so hard

It's hard to have the power to throw

Or hide.

We have balloons in all colors

Filled in all sizes

By days end, we are soaked

Drying off, picking up all the little

Pieces of what was once balloons

Filled with water;

Fun to remember.

CURIOSITY

Getting the better of me

I always want to discover things

Finding out brings

Trouble to me.

It's like yesterday

My mom was reading the newspaper

Bears love bird seeds

Now, how is that possible

Big black bears

Eat bird seeds meant for little

Tiny hummingbirds

Does not make sense.

Besides, I see birds every day

Although I live on the edge of

The woods by the Appalachian Mountains

In North Carolina, I have yet to see a black bear.

I have been told they are four to seven feet tall

I wonder how much does one weigh?

My dad weighs a hundred ninety-seven pounds

He is six feet one.

Maybe, that's what the black bear weighs.

I want to see a bear

Curiosity tells me to overload the

Bird feeder with birdseeds.

Well, on Saturday only birds came by

No bears.

On Sunday, you guessed it

A cute little black bear

Maybe two feet tall

Smaller than I am

Eating the bird seeds that have fallen to the ground.

I go get Mom and her phone

To take a picture.

While focusing the camera

The big black bear I wanted to see

Comes up right behind the baby.

I was so scared, I could not move

I mean not even able to run back in the house

No picture

Too scared to move

Frozen.

I WOULD LOVE TO

See a rat laugh

I guess he does all the time

It's just I do not see him.

He runs away

As soon as my mom sees him.

She screams so loud you

Would think a monster gator

Was in the room with her

Not a tiny furry rat

Whom I would love to see laugh

Giggle when my mom runs away

From the tiny furry rat.

THE TREE AND THE BENCH

While hanging on high in the tree

Men on the bench

I listen to them talk

I guess they know I am in the tree

They are comparing the list of things they need to buy

Both are getting tuna fish, bread and onions.

I am not an onion person

I love cucumbers

One of my favorites.

The men on the bench speak

The sun is shining and it's very hot today

I wonder if the moon will be as bright tonight as it was last night

Did you see the moon?

Wow, it was spectacular.

Funny, all these years

We talk about a man in the moon

I have seen the craters

It certainly looks like a person up there

My thinking is, that it belongs to a woman

Not a man

Big mistake

It's a woman in the moon

For sure.

Two men agreeing

On the park bench.

COLOR

The ladybug
Any color you want
You're the artist.
Never seen an orange ladybug?
Go for it
It's bright orange
Easy to spot on the green leaf.
Now it's time for a purple
Apple, I love my new tree
Filled with purple apples
That taste sweet like
Chocolate candy.
The fun of being the artist
Like a cook, make anything you want
The way you want.
My world strange to all

Yet, fun in the making

Green tigers

Yellow elephants

Blue sun

Red alligators.

BOOKS

Not sure I like reading

It's just I like going to

So many places

That books take me.

Oh, the fun I have had reading about

Scary monsters

Boys getting into trouble exploring

The high seas.

I read and learn about the hot sun

Inventors that tried to fly

With such success.

The stories which are true

About landing on the moon

Taking one giant step for all of us.

The busy bees

The ugly teeth of witches, that fly in the night.

The pretty fairy godmother that helps you find

What you're looking for

I learned the magic of magic wands

Oh, what fun to have your own magic wand

I have learned through books

Best to work for what you want

Magic wands only in books.

MY DOG

Out runs me

I chase him down my street

When he stops to smell the grass

I catch up to him.

My cheeks are rosy from running so fast

I pet his warm moist nose

Asking, why do you run from me

Do you not know I like being with you?

If you're interested in exploring

Know that I want to explore with you

All the fun and sights we can enjoy

Together.

He is happy when I talk softly to him

I can tell, his tail is wagging

Faster than he ran.

FISHING

When I was a kid

Living in New York City

We would go to Central Park.

This park was really big

Like all the buildings in New York;

Everything is big there.

This park has lakes, rocks to climb

Kids playing baseball

Grownups riding horses

Moms pushing babies

In all kinds of carriages

People walk their dogs with little

Mittens on their paws

I guess to keep them warm.

Today, Dad was taking me fishing

In Central Park at one of the lakes

I do not have a fishing pole

Dad helps me make one.

With a large jar

We tie on three strings

Around the part of the jar that has ridges
Where the top of the jar twists on;
The ridges hold the string.
Each string is about three feet long
I can hang over the side of
The lake and catch
Tiny tadpoles.
I dip the jar in the water
Wait and dream until
The fish enters the jar
I pick up the jar
And there are three
Tiny fish.
I can look at them
Breathe
Chase each other.
I go back to the lake and catch a few more
Within an hour, I have about twenty
In my fishing jar.
At one time the jar held mayonnaise
Now it's home to all these

Tiny fish.

I get a bit tired

Not sure what to do with them.

My dog looks at what's in the jar

I think he may want to eat them

No way.

I just put them back in the water

While my dog barks.

BORED

I hate the word

There is so much in life to do

The word

Gives me a feeling of laziness

Lacks interest

Run away from life

Bored.

Find something to do

Instead of wishing your life away

Even if it's a walk around the block.

Try

Keeping busy with things you love

Seeking purpose for your passions

Exploring your neighborhood;

Good times awaits

Life

Snuggle, play, giggle.

THERE IS A ROACH ON THE FLOOR

I have left it there for three days

Waiting for Mom or Dad to pick it up.

Well, she did it today

Finally, that ugly roach is in the garbage.

I do not like roaches

What have they done to get such a bad rap?

They come out of hiding

In the night

It's possible we do not like roaches

For they are creatures of the night.

I do not see them often

When I do

I try to kill them

Not catch them.

I stomp on them

If I miss

I jump like

A grasshopper

Jump high

Almost falling on myself.

I do not want to touch

Even though I have on these big, thick, black sneakers

Pick my foot up to stomp the roach

It moves faster than I can

Stomp.

Runs behind the refrigerator

Looking for food

Water

Something.

The roach of the night

Came for a visit and

Now

Lies dead on the floor

From my stomp.

I hate the idea of its guts

On the bottom of my shoe

New problem

Guts from the roach.

Maybe I will go outside and clean off my

Sneaker by swishing it over the grass

Hopefully someone will pick up

What remains

Dad will, for sure

He hates roaches more than I do.

SCARED

I am scared tonight

Dad comes to my rescue

Dad is fearless

Always.

Dad tells me it is okay

To fear the dark

We cannot see

Everything there is to see

Yet, we hear everything

In this room of mine.

In dark

We do not see

What we hear

Fear grows.

Dad

Turn on the light

Okay to fear a little

Every now and then.

TODAY I WANT

To learn how to sew

I like buttons

I am going to

Sew on buttons

From my mom's sewing box.

There so many colors of buttons

Tiny, little white ones

Like I see every day on Dad's shirts.

The best are the ones Mom took off her dress

They are red, big and look

Like a happy face.

I watch how Mom sews

I try to follow her

The first step

Getting thread in the needle

Not sure you know this

The hole for the thread

Is tiny;

Matter of fact, it's smaller than the thread.

How can one do this?

I try and try

I just get tired

Before I sew on my first button.

Mom

To the rescue

She has a little plastic box

With needles already threaded

In that tiny hole

Ready to go, she tells me

Yes, great invention.

YOU'RE LOOKING AT ME

I want you to find me pretty

For I am not a flower

I am a lady bug.

Happy as can be

Flying from one flower

To the next

Quiet as a cat.

Often, I get by

No one sees me move

Once in a while

I hear a sound

For those that find me

Right in front of them

Happy to see this pretty

Lady bug

On a warm summer's day.

A NEW RESPONSIBILITY

I want the dog in the window

It's so cute and cuddly

Dad, can we have the puppy?

No, it's too much work.

No Daddy, I will do everything

Please Daddy

Can we just go inside?

I want to at least hold the puppy.

I hold the puppy

He's like I thought

The puppy fills my hands

He starts to lick my palm

As if he is reading our future

I start laughing

It tickles.

Can you just imagine

Every day he licks my hand

It tickles and I laugh.

Somehow

Daddy agrees with me

He buys the puppy.

I promise to do everything

Feed him each day

Bathe him when he needs it

Teach him to go to the bathroom outside

Most important of all, walk him each day

Of course, I have to give him a name.

Easy, I will name him Tickles.

Two weeks go by

I am getting yelled at every minute of

Every day

Did you feed Tickles today?

Of course, I did not

Did you take Tickles for a walk?

If course, I did not

I hear my name the loudest when

Mom yells

"David, Tickles went to the bathroom

Pick it up right this minute"

How am I going to take care of Tickles

It's so hard

Except the licking of my hand

Still tickles.

PLANTING MARIGOLDS

My cutie

Five-year-old

Joanna and I, going

Into nature to do a tiny bit of

Gardening.

We bring home twelve little marigold plants

They are going to be planted

We begin our work

In two large planters in front of our home.

Shovel in hand

Holes dug

Dirt all over us

The enjoyment being

With Joanna, twelve marigolds

Dirt, shovels, gloves and

Nature.

Our marigolds start to talk with us

As we watch them grow;

Life at its best.

WITHIN THE SAND DUNE

I see something moving slowly

An egg hatching

Life

Emerging baby turtles

Squirming for the sea, in bright sun light

Dodging birds in flight.

Run fast as I can

Little help for tiny baby turtles

From those birds I chase away

No place to hide.

By afternoon baby turtles at sea

For sure, some are saved

You know what scares me?

Every year turtles need help

Even when I'm not there.

SUNDAE

I want to learn how to make one

I know there is no school

For sundaes.

Can I ask my teacher

One day to teach us

How to make a sundae?

Like Jillian's Ice Cream Shop

Maybe we can go on a field trip

To the ice cream store

The whole class can watch

The ice cream man make a sundae

Right in front of us

Not behind the counter, away from us.

For me

I would ask for three scoops

Mom and Dad never get one

For themselves.

If I have three scoops

I can share the sundae

I like vanilla ice cream

Three scoops first in my dish.

Next

I would ask for hot chocolate syrup,

Lots of whip cream

As high as he can go

At least three times the

Regular amount.

The top of all this good stuff

Seven sweet cherries

With the stem still intact

To make it easy to pick up.

I raise my hand

Call out

Miss Sherry, Miss Sherry

Can we go to

“Sundae school?”

WATERMELON

It's a hot day

So very hot

I hate to be outside

Mom calls

She has watermelon.

We run to greet

The watermelon

There are eight of us

Mom makes nine slices.

There is enough for all of us

How does she do it?

Mom divides the watermelon

All have a big slice

The slice I have seems

To be the same size

As all the others.

Cold watermelon on a hot day

The perfect mom

How did she know?

WHAT TO CHOOSE

I am often asked

What animal would I be

If I had to choose?

I would rather be me

But they said if you had to choose

I think I would go for big animals

Like tigers

Elephants

Gorillas

All animals of the jungle.

All animals I have not seen except in

Zoos.

No zoos for me

If I was a tiger.

Elouan
I'm a hybrid
"Who am I?"
I'm a Pig

MOM

Can you read me a story?

I love sitting in bed

With Mom at my side

She is reading to me

Just me

After her busy day.

Sometimes, I like her reading to me

So I can stay up later

Or ask her questions

About the book.

The best books are about

Strange animals.

Some of them she hates

They look ugly, I like that

Little animals learn from their moms

Just like I do.

Tonight, she is reading the story about

"Time for School"

How a baby otter learns to swim from his mom.

Mom is teaching me to swim

I like the cool water

But I hate getting my face wet

When she wants me to go underwater.

Mom has me pick up the baby plastic otters she has

Thrown in the water

I do it.

It's hard

So many things to think about

Keep my eyes open underwater

I have to shut my mouth

I hate to drink the pool water

Then, I have to grab the otters

Before I choke.

Last, I have to come up

Out of the water for air.

The book is finished

She fixes the blanket

Gives me the gentle kiss goodnight

Shuts the light.

I dream of swimming across the pool

From end to end.

QUESTIONS

Asked all the time

I just want to know

Everything

So many new things

I see

I hear.

I love learning

About the sea

That looks like it comes to an end

I wonder will I fall off.

Papouli, my grandfather, tells me

"No".

"You see, the world is round like a ball

You cannot fall off, you can

Keep walking, sailing, riding your bike

Around and around", he said.

"Before we knew the world was round

You could look out to sea and

It did look like somehow we might fall off

Yet you never will."

I think I understand now

Knowing people who did not know

The earth was round and

Feared the sea.

I need to think about this for a while

I look out to sea and

I think

I may find

The edge to fall from.

IGUANA

No one in my home

Likes iguanas.

They look like dragons

They eat the leaves on

Mom's favorite

Hibiscus plant

Especially the red flowers.

One day, while reading

In my hammock

Gus came along

I caught him

Maybe he let me catch him

He likes me

I can tell

He sits quietly with me.

Now

He is hiding with me in my room

I found a great big box

For his new home

We can visit each other all the time.

Make no mistake

He can scare anyone he wants

With me, he lets me pet him

I feed him

A few leaves from Mom's plant.

We get to have talks together

I sit in the hammock

With Gus

We tell each other about

Our dreams.

Today, I told him

Of my trip to

The beach

We swam

Ate on a blanket

Rode waves.

I told Gus he did not come along because

I didn't know if he would like

The long car ride to the beach

I knew for sure, he would not like the peanut butter

Sandwich.

I think Gus knows he is best

Waiting at home for me.

He tells me, "If anyone

Saw me they would only scream."

He is best waiting for me at home

Safely hidden in my room

A danger to no one.

SATURDAY FIRE

Next to my home

There is an empty lot

On Saturdays

Mom and Dad are busy

Cleaning

Shopping

Relaxing

Fixing our home.

Sometimes, I have to help

I do help

As fast as I can

I want to get back to

My forest

Always waiting for me

Right next to my home.

I enter

Two or three steps

On the trail I have made

I cannot see my house

I am alone.

The path I built

With my two friends

Jennifer and Christopher

We go around the neighborhood

Pick up things from the trash piles

For our trail, which

It's so very hard to find.

The trail leads us to our fort

We built against a tree

With all the palms we have collected.

It's pretty safe

Except for the iguanas

They are like dragons in my stories

Just smaller

Just as scary

They sneak up on you.

We talk of plans

School and the rains that may come

For our fort does get wet when

A storm comes through.

The rain at times destroys all

Our books and drawings and

Pillows.

Lucky for us, no rain

Jennifer and Christopher join me this Saturday

Today, I brought matches with me

I found a tin box at the neighbor's trash pile

Filled with matches.

I love fire

Today, I light one with the help of my friends

We are not cold

We just pretend we need warmth from the fire

Somehow, it got out of hand.

Maybe we just kept adding

Too many dry twigs

The fire got bigger and bigger.

We tried to stomp the fire out

Everything we collected

Was going up in flames

The fire grew

Before we realized it

Our books were on fire too.

We decided to run

Running didn't help

The fire continued

We sat in our front yard

And watched.

We did not know what to do

Most important, we did not want to get in trouble.

We lost enough

Our fort was burning up

Someone knew what to do.

We heard a firetruck

Four firemen got the hoses

Attached them to the fire hydrant;

They worked very fast.

All the neighbors were watching

Talking about how close the fire came to their homes;

When the fire was out

Nothing was left except burnt trunks of trees.

Christopher looked at me

He wondered should we tell them?

I shrug my shoulders

I really do not know

Jennifer says, no I do not want to get in trouble.

The firemen talk to the neighbors

It's been very dry and the fire could have started

From all the dry leaves.

We saw no sign of wrong-doing

Although we saw signs of someone

Camping out.

Christopher, Jennifer, and I look at each other

We are happy, no wrong-doing

That means us.

When the firemen leave

The neighbors return to their homes

Except

My aunt Melissa.

She looked at the three of us

“I know you did this”, she said

“You’re lucky the firemen said

No wrong-doing.

You should have gotten into trouble.”

We didn’t.

The fire filled us with fear

The excitement, the loss of our fort

More important, the loss of our forest.

Wish I had a picture

Of all the excitement

In what was lost.

FIRST BOX OF CRAYONS

My new toy

All the colors

Yellow, purple

Blue

Orange

All with sharp points.

I can make a rainbow

A palm tree

Draw my home

With my family inside.

Mom hates when the crayons break

I stick them up my nose

A very big sneeze

Got the purple crayon

Out of my nose.

Mom said no more crayons

Unless I never put them back

In my nose.

I want my crayons

My nose did not like

The purple crayon.

I tell Mom

“Mom, I want my crayons back please

No more purple crayon in my nose.”

Crayons back, yes.

SIX ORANGE HORSES

What a sight

They are very big

Like my dad's foot.

One came up to me

I wanted to touch

The orange horses

I waited

Wanted to make sure

He wanted me to touch him too.

Gently, I put my hand on his long face

Oh, how wonderful the orange horse felt

Soft and fuzzy.

Delighted we are

As the other five orange horses

Slowly

Come close to join our

Delight.

SUNDAY DINNER

The family is all

Sitting around the table

Mom cooked lemon-baked chicken

And potatoes;

One of the best meals.

I stretch to pick up the salad plate

I tip over my dad's glass of wine

As quick as I can, I pick the glass up

A bit too late, some of the wine

Spilled over on to the table.

I am waiting for the scream

How could you?

You're clumsy

Can't you watch what you're doing?

Instead, my

Papouli (grandfather in Greek) said

“Wow, your nickname should be Ninja

You were so fast to pick up the glass

Look how much is left in the glass.”

I couldn’t believe my mistake

Made me feel good

Only my papouli would come up

With something good.

Thank you Papouli!

We both felt good about something

Gone wrong.

MY COUSIN

Wins tournaments

Catching sailfish.

Can you imagine

Catching the beautiful

Blue, fast swimming sailfish

At the rate of

Seventy miles an hour?

Jumping ten to twenty feet in the air

Called

Dancing on the sea's surface.

Weighing hundreds of pounds

With its dorsal fin, we all recognize

As its sail.

My cousin

Often sends me pictures

Going out to sea early in the morning

Sunrise as his companion.

It's the second day of the tournament

The first day is setting up

All the equipment

Catching bait called goggle eyes

Yes, the bait has big glassy eyes.

My cousin tells me the sailfish can change

Colors right before his eyes

Possibly just before they latch on to goggle eyes.

Sailfish will always be back for another day

In all tournaments

Catch and release, rule number one;

Rule number two

Win.

Made in the USA
Columbia, SC
16 December 2023

28557253R10077